W9-ADW-334

LEARNING COMMONS
CAYUGA
COMMUNITY COLLEGE
FULTON, NEW YORK 13069

Girls Play to Win

HOCKEY

by Dave McMahon

Content Consultant
Angela Ruggiero
U.S. Olympic
Hockey Player

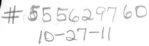

#555629760
10-27-11

NORWOOD HOUSE PRESS
CHICAGO, ILLINOIS

Norwood House Press
P.O. Box 316598
Chicago, Illinois 60631

For information regarding Norwood House Press, please visit our website at
www.norwoodhousepress.com or call 866-565-2900.

David Stoecklein/Photolibrary, cover, 1; Joseph Gareri/iStockphoto, cover, 1; iStock-photo, cover, 1; Chris O'Meara/AP Images, 4, 42; James Boulette/iStockphoto, 6, 23; Bigstock, 8, 21; Shutterstock Images, 9; Jonathan Larsen/Shutterstock Images, 11, 45, 47; Fotolia, 13, 24; Michael Braun/iStockphoto, 14; Scott Gardner/AP Images, 15; St. Paul Pioneer Press, 16; Tony Campbell/Shutterstock Images, 18; Minnesota Historical Society, 19; Michael Braun/iStockphoto, 25; Kevork Djansezian/AP Images, 29, 41; Denis Paquin/AP Images, 30; Johnny Lye/Shutterstock Images, 33; Jonas Ekstromer/AP Images, 35; Sergei Bachlakov/Shutterstock Images, 36; Denis Paquin/AP Images, 39; Jussi Nukari/AP Images, 48; Paul Drinkwater/NBCU Photo Bank/AP Images, 51; Mike Webber/iStockphoto, 55; Jeff Wheeler/AP Images, 57; Dave McMahon, 64 (top); USA Hockey/Nancie Battagliam 64 (bottom)

Editor: Chrös McDougall
Designer: Christa Schneider
Project Management: Red Line Editorial

Library of Congress Cataloging-in-Publication Data

McMahon, Dave.
  Girls play to win hockey / by Dave McMahon.
    p. cm. — (Girls play to win hockey)
  Includes bibliographical references and index.
  Summary: "Covers the history, rules, fundamentals and significant personalities of the sport of women's hockey. Topics include: techniques, strategies, competitive events, and equipment. Glossary, Additional Resources and Index included"—Provided by publisher.
  ISBN-13: 978-1-59953-390-2 (library edition : alk. paper)
  ISBN-10: 1-59953-390-1 (library edition : alk. paper)
  1. Women hockey players—Juvenile literature. I. Title.
  GV848.6.W65M36 2010
  796.962082–dc22
                        2010009811

©2011 by Norwood House Press.
All rights reserved.
No part of this book may be reproduced without written permission from the publisher.

Manufactured in the United States of America in North Mankato, Minnesota.
157N—072010

Girls Play to Win
HOCKEY

Table of Contents

▲ *Angela Ruggiero scores against China in the 2010 Olympics.*

CHAPTER 1

HOCKEY
BASICS

Girls' hockey was not a common sport when Jenny Potter and Angela Ruggiero were growing up. When Angela began playing at age seven, she had to play on a boys' team. It was the same for Jenny, who began playing organized hockey in eighth grade. But that did not slow these girls down. When women's hockey **debuted** in the 1998 Olympic Winter Games, Jenny and Angela were there, playing for Team USA.

Potter began skating at age two, but she actually played on a boys' football team before joining her first hockey team. Once she began focusing on hockey, it was a fast road to success. In 1995, a 16-year-old Potter first tried out for Team USA. She made the team in 1997, and went on to star for Team USA and also the University of Minnesota Duluth.

Ruggiero was known by her teammates to be a hard worker. She showed that in college. Ruggiero was a star player for Harvard University. She then graduated with honors. Her hard work showed with the national team, too. Ruggiero was later named the top **defensewoman** in the Olympics twice. She also took home the same honor in the World Women's Championship four times.

Twelve years after the 1998 Olympics, Potter and Ruggiero still had not slowed down. The two youngest members of the 1998 U.S. women's hockey team were the two oldest members of the 2010 team. The four-time Olympians starred, helping Team USA win a silver medal.

GETTING STARTED

Hockey is a high-energy sport that focuses on teamwork. Some girls want to play hockey in the Olympics or for a college team. Others just want to skate a few times a year and play with their friends at a local **rink** or on a pond. Whether at the Olympics or in a backyard pond, ice hockey games can be action-packed.

▲ *Olympians inspire girls like this one to go out and play.*

The object of the game is simple. Two teams compete to put a **puck** into the other team's net. If they succeed, the team has scored a goal. The players move the puck by hitting it with their **hockey sticks**. Whichever team has more goals at the end is the winner.

A PLACE TO PLAY

Official hockey games often take place at an indoor ice rink. These rinks have walls called **boards** around the outside. By containing the puck, the walls keep the action going. There are also lines painted into the ice that indicate the different zones and where **face-offs** take place.

Some official ice rinks are outside, too. These rinks are similar to indoor rinks. The main difference is that the players are exposed to the weather. That means players sometimes have to deal with the snow or other elements. Outdoor ice is often bumpy. It can also become wet or slushy if the weather warms up. Playing on frozen creeks, ponds, and lakes is also an option. Just make certain an adult has checked that the water is frozen and safe to skate on.

MAKING A TEAM

A team can have six players on the ice at the same time. Each person plays one of the following positions: **goaltender**, left or right defensewoman, left wing, center, and right wing. The goaltender has the important

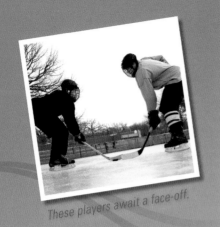

These players await a face-off.

FACE-OFFS

Face-offs are used to start or restart the action in a hockey game. The centers from each team line up on opposite sides of the dot at the center of the circle. The hockey official, or referee, then drops the puck. Each team's center tries to get control of the puck or pass it to a teammate. There are five circles and nine spots on the ice where face-offs occur. Face-offs happen at the start of each period, after a goal or penalty, or any other time that the referee has to stop the game.

job of keeping the puck from entering her team's goal. The defensewomen try to keep the opposing players away from their goal. Each winger generally stays on her side of the ice—left or right—and tries to score goals. The center takes face-offs and also tries to score goals. Collectively, the wings and center are known as **forwards**. The forwards and defensewomen are all responsible for playing offense and defense. All of the players have to **back-check** to defend their goal against the opponents.

MOVING ON THE ICE

The first step to hockey is the skating. A hockey player needs to be able to skate quickly so she can move across the ice. Players must also know how to skate backward and to make quick turns. It is important for skaters to

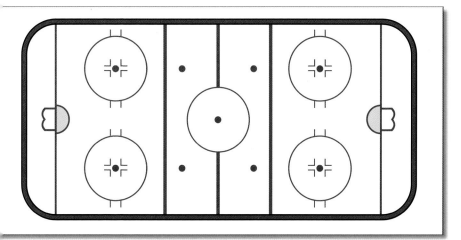

▲ *This drawing shows the layout of the hockey rink, including the face-off circles, red lines and blue lines, and the goal creases.*

stay low while skating. This gives the skater more power while also helping her maintain balance.

Skaters can turn quickly by using the edges of their skates. Each skate blade has an inside and outside edge. By leaning on the inside edge of one skate and the outside edge of another, the skater can turn quickly. A crossover turn is another good way to change directions. To do this, the skater leans in one direction and crosses one skate over the other. The inside skate uses the outside edge of the blade while the outside skate uses the inside edge.

Stopping is an important element of the game, too. A hockey stop allows a player to stop quickly. To do it, the player digs the edges of both skates into the ice at the same time. The edges push against the ice like a snow-plow until the player stops. Sometimes the skates will make specks of ice fly into the air.

After learning to skate, a player must learn to handle a hockey stick. This lets her keep control of the puck while skating. A player controls the puck by tapping it back and forth with the blade. She can use the inside (**forehand**) or outside (**backhand**) of the blade while stick handling.

Although stick handling is important, players also need to pass the puck to their teammates. Passing helps a team get around defenders and set up goals. A good

The Equipment

As with any sport, having the appropriate equipment is key to performance and protection. Finding the right skates is important. There are two kinds of ice skates. Skates that have pointed edges on the front tip of the blade are made for figure skating. They do not work well for playing hockey. Hockey skates have a smooth blade and a thicker boot than figure skates.

Having proper protection is particularly important in hockey. The sport should never be played without a mouth guard, gloves, elbow pads, and shin pads. It is also never acceptable to play without a helmet. The helmet can help prevent a concussion if a player falls to the ice and bangs her head. In addition, the helmet has a face mask or shield to provide protection from flying pucks and high sticks. Players also need hockey pants (called breezers), hockey socks, and pelvic protectors.

▲ *Canada's Gillian Apps handles the puck in the 2006 Olympics.*

passer can find her teammate on the move. To do that, she has to aim the pass toward the open space ahead of the receiver. If the pass is timed just right, the puck and the player will meet at the same time. On good hockey teams, the players are always moving and looking for this open space to receive a pass.

The final step in offense is shooting. There are two primary ways to shoot: the wrist **shot** and the slap shot. The wrist shot is more common. To take a wrist shot, the player steadies the stick with her top hand and flicks her other wrist. This turns the blade of the stick and drives the puck forward.

Slap shots are mostly used when a player has time and space. To do one, the player winds up. Then, when the stick blade comes back down to the puck, the player rolls her wrist and "slaps" the puck. She then follows through, with the stick ultimately aiming back at the target.

TENDING THE NET

The goaltender is the final line of defense for a hockey team. She has to stand in front of the goal and try to block the shots from going past her. The goalie is noticeable because she wears more equipment than the other players. This includes two large leg pads that are used to block shots. She also has a glove, a **blocker**, a larger stick, and skates that allow her to move more freely.

The Superman Dive

Because falling is part of hockey, an advantage often goes to the player who can get up more quickly than the opponent. An exercise that helps players to get off the ice quickly is the Superman dive. To do it, skaters simply skate for six or seven strides, bend their knees, and jump onto the ice with their arms extended— picture Superman flying. After sliding for a second or two, they hop back up as quickly as they can and continue to skate.

▲ Ice sprays up from under this girl's skates as she performs a hockey stop.

The offensive player will get a point if she scores a goal.

HOCKEY LINGO

Assist: *Credit given to the two players who most recently passed the puck to the goal scorer.*

Penalty box: *An enclosed area where a player sits if she has been charged with a penalty.*

Penalty kill: *When a team is playing shorthanded due to a player receiving a penalty.*

Point: *A goal or an assist.*

Power play: *When the opposing team is down a player because she received a penalty and has to spend time in the penalty box.*

The goalie often uses her body to stop shots. She can defend a low shot by dropping to the ice and sticking out one of the leg pads. She can stop high shots by either catching them with her glove or knocking them out of the way with her blocker. She can also absorb shots into her chest or bat them away with her stick. After a goalie stops a shot, her team will try to get the puck so it can go on offense.

There is only one rule difference between men's and women's hockey. Women are not allowed to body check at any level. Checking is when a player uses her body, such as her hip or shoulder, to stop an opponent who has control of the puck. If a player does check, she is charged with a two-minute **penalty**.

Once the team is in place, it's time to play hockey!

▲ Hockey goalies, like Canada's Shannon Szabados, wear lots of pads.

▲ *These schoolgirls play hockey in St. Paul, Minnesota, in 1925.*

CHAPTER 2

HISTORY
OF THE GAME

Women's hockey first appeared about 30 years after the game was created. In the 1880s, Lord and Lady Stanley invited men and women to play alongside each other at their home in Canada. Lord Stanley's daughter, Isobel, became one of the first female hockey players in Canada. Before long, hockey was being played elsewhere in Canada, too. The *Ottawa Citizen* newspaper reported that a women's hockey game took place in Barrie, Ontario, Canada, in 1892.

The sport of ice hockey developed quickly in the last half of that century. In a matter of decades, it had grown to be a popular activity worldwide. A group of men in Kingston, Ontario, Canada, reportedly played the very first hockey game in 1855. By 1879, students at McGill University in Montreal, Canada, were playing, too. In 1893, hockey was reported in the United States. The **National Hockey League (NHL)** was formed in 1917.

The first women's hockey league was created in 1900. It had three teams and was based in Quebec. The teams' uniforms were very different from those worn by women's teams today. The players all wore long woolen skirts. Goaltenders turned the dresses into an advantage by sewing buckshot pellets, or large balls of lead, into the hemlines. The extra weight at the bottom of the dress allowed them to use the dress to keep pucks from going between their legs.

The Stanley Cup

Lord Stanley was Canada's sixth governor general. He supported women playing hockey. But he is best known for his contribution to men's hockey. He donated what became known as the Stanley Cup. It was a silver bowl awarded to the top men's **amateur** team in Canada. Today, it is given to the champion of the NHL's Stanley Cup playoffs.

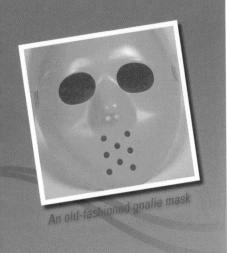
An old-fashioned goalie mask

GOALIE MASKS

Elizabeth Graham was a goaltender at Queens University in Kingston, Ontario, Canada. She is credited with being the first goaltender, man or woman, to wear a mask in an organized game. A Montreal, Canada, newspaper reported that Graham wore a fencing mask in a game in 1927. In the NHL, goalie Jacques Plante was the first to use a mask, in 1959.

IN THE UNITED STATES

Women's hockey began to be played in the United States around the same time it appeared in Canada. Women were photographed playing hockey in Alaska in 1892. A report in the *Ottawa Citizen* described a game between two women's teams in 1899 at the Ice Palace in Philadelphia, Pennsylvania.

Colleges have played an important role in developing women's hockey in the United States. In 1908, a women's hockey team was playing at the University of Alaska, although the university did not officially recognize the team. Other U.S. colleges and universities began creating women's hockey teams around 1910. Records kept by the University of Minnesota show that women played organized hockey in 1916. By

▲ *These women played hockey for the University of Minnesota in 1925.*

1932, Carleton College in Northfield, Minnesota, had two women's teams. The school had no men's team. But those teams slowly disappeared as the country hit the Great Depression in the 1930s and World War II in the 1940s.

It was not until 1964 that women's hockey returned to the college level. Brown University in Rhode Island formed a team that year. Three years later, Brown began competing against universities from Canada. Cornell University in New York added a team in 1972. Others soon began popping up after that.

Ringette

Before women's hockey became widely popular in the United States, some women played ringette. The sport was created in 1963 and is similar to hockey in that it is played on ice with sticks. But ringette involves more passing and team play than hockey. Instead of a puck, the game centers on a ring that is approximately 6.5 inches (16.5 cm) in diameter. Players pass the ring by stabbing their flat-ended stick through the middle of it as it slides to them on the ice. The sport is still played in some countries, but it is especially popular in Canada. According to Ringette Canada, the national governing body for the sport, there are more than 50,000 participants in the country.

SEEING GROWTH

In 1972, U.S. Congress passed legislation known as Title IX. After that, all federally funded activities and programs had to give equal treatment to men and women. Today, most people know of Title IX because of its effect on sports. Title IX meant that public schools and universities had to add more women's sports teams. Hockey was one of several sports that U.S. colleges added for female athletes as a result of the legislation.

Brown had fielded a women's hockey team before Title IX. But in 1975, it became the first university to make

▲ *Sports became more accessible for girls when Title IX passed.*

women's hockey a varsity sport. Three other colleges in the northeast began offering athletic scholarships in 1981. They were Providence College in Rhode Island, the University of New Hampshire, and Northeastern University in Massachusetts.

College hockey has continued to grow since then. The first National Collegiate Athletic Association (NCAA) championship was held in 2001. One year later, the University of Minnesota opened Ridder Arena. It was the first arena built specifically for a women's college hockey team. Since hockey is most popular in places that have cold winters, it is found mostly at northern colleges.

GOING INTERNATIONAL

Women's hockey took its first major step on the international sporting landscape in 1990. That is when the International Ice Hockey Federation (IIHF) held the first World Women's Championship. Eight years later, women's hockey became part of the Olympics. Participation levels have consistently risen as the U.S. national team has had success and exposure at the World Women's Championship and the Olympic Winter Games.

International Competitions

IIHF World Women's Championship

First Tournament: 1990

Frequency: Every non-Olympic year

Most Successful Team: Canada (9 gold, 3 silver medals)

Olympic Games

First Tournament: 1998

Frequency: Every four years

Most Successful Team: Canada (3 gold, 1 silver medal)

More girls are playing hockey than ever before.

RISE IN NUMBERS

USA Hockey is the national governing body for all ice hockey in the United States. The organization has seen its number of registered female players grow as women's hockey has made strides in international competition.

Only 6,336 women were registered with USA Hockey as playing on a team in 1990. The number of female players increased to 10,416 during the 1992–93 season. By 2009, female membership with USA Hockey grew to nearly 60,000 players. And that does not include high school and college players, who do not need to be registered with USA Hockey. In Minnesota alone, which is a state known for ice hockey, there are 200 high schools and 23 colleges that support girls' and women's teams. Those teams in Minnesota account for approximately 5,000 players not registered with USA Hockey.

Hockey remains one of the fastest growing women's sports in the United States.

▲ *The U.S. national team has inspired young girls like these to start playing hockey.*

CHAPTER 3

TAKING
THE LEAD

The growth of girls' and women's hockey eventually resulted in a U.S. national team. The first U.S. national women's ice hockey team was formed in 1987. To build the team, the Amateur Hockey Association of the United States held tryout camps in Massachusetts, New York, Michigan, and Minnesota, states known for hockey. It was not long before Team USA had one of its first star players.

PLAYING WITH BOYS

Cammi Granato came from a hockey-loving family. As a matter of fact, Granato's parents went to a Chicago Blackhawks hockey game on their first date. The family's backyard in Downers Grove, Illinois, proved to be the perfect training ground for their daughter.

Starting at the age of five, Granato would skate on the backyard rink her father created every winter. Over the years, she developed her skating and stick-handling skills. She also developed a passion for the game, which she played with her brothers.

When Granato grew up in the 1970s and 1980s, there were no girls' teams in her area. So she joined a boys' hockey team. Many early players on the U.S. women's ice hockey team played on boys'

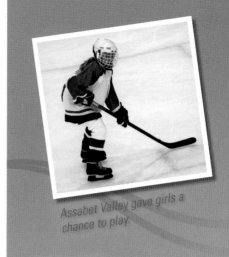

Assabet Valley gave girls a chance to play.

ASSABET VALLEY

When a local girl in Concord, Massachusetts, wanted to play for a boys' team, Carl Gray founded the Assabet Valley girls' ice hockey program in 1972 to provide girls an opportunity to play hockey with other girls. The team has been very successful. It has won 39 USA Hockey National Championship tournaments and finished second 27 times. Assabet teams have also won 108 state and regional championships. Carl Gray and his son, Eric, were assistant coaches of the first U.S. national team. The team competed in the World Invitational Tournament in 1987.

teams because their options were to either play on a boys' team or not play the sport at all. Granato played on a boys' team until her junior year in high school. By then, the boys had grown bigger and stronger than her.

After leaving the boys' team, Granato tried playing other sports. But hockey would be part of her future. Providence College in Rhode Island offered her a scholarship to play on its women's hockey team. She joined the team in 1989. The college hockey teams in the northeast provided many players for the early national teams. Granato was one of these players. She made the U.S. women's hockey team in 1990.

Granato's talent quickly became apparent as she developed into a star on the national team. When women's hockey debuted in the 1998 Olympics, Granato was

Family Affair

Cammi Granato was not the only standout ice hockey player in her family. Her brother, Tony, had an excellent playing career in the NHL. He went on to become an NHL coach. Another brother, Don, had a successful career playing minor league hockey and also became a coach. A third brother, Rob, was a captain when he played hockey for the University of Wisconsin.

the team captain and the face of U.S. women's hockey. She led Team USA to win the Olympic gold medal in 1998. It was the first Olympic gold medal ever awarded in women's hockey.

Passing on the NHL

Cammi Granato was invited to training camp in 1997 with the NHL's New York Islanders. She declined the offer. Granato was wary of the attention it would attract. Also, she did not think she was physically big enough to compete on the men's team.

Granato became one of the most recognizable female athletes in the United States. She was chosen to carry the U.S. flag at the closing ceremony of the 1998 Olympics. She was even featured on Wheaties cereal boxes.

The 1998 Olympic gold medal gained Granato fame. But it was hardly her only accomplishment. Gold, silver, and bronze medals are also given out at the World Women's Championship. She had already helped Team USA win the silver medal at the World Women's Championship four times. She would later help Team USA win four more silver medals in the World Women's Championship. Granato followed her gold at the 1998 Olympics in Nagano, Japan, with a silver medal at the 2002 Olympic

Winter Games in Salt Lake City, Utah. She was also a member of the gold-medal team at the 2005 World Women's Championships.

Granato's career ended in 2006 when she did not make the Olympic team that competed in Turin, Italy. But she completed her career as the all-time scoring leader in international tournament competition. After retiring, Granato worked as a women's hockey television reporter for NBC at the 2006 and 2010 Olympic Winter Games. She also worked as a radio broadcaster for the Los Angeles Kings of the NHL. In 2008, she became the first woman to be inducted into the U.S. Hockey Hall of Fame.

Players such as Granato helped make women's hockey more accessible. Today, most girls who want to play ice hockey can play on girls' teams. The best players can compete internationally on the biggest stage.

▲ Cammi Granato (left) and Karyn Bye showed off their gold medals from the 1998 Olympics.

▲ *Karyn Bye was a star player for Team USA during the 1990s.*

CHAPTER 4

WORLD
CHAMPIONS

Women's hockey was growing around the world during the 1980s. In 1987, the Ontario Women's Hockey Association held the first World Invitational Tournament. It was the top international women's hockey tournament at the time. But the IIHF had bigger ideas. It soon began planning a true world championship event for women's hockey.

That dream came true in 1990. The first IIHF World Women's Championships took place that year in Ottawa, Ontario.

The Olympic Winter Games are held every four years. Today, the World Women's Championship takes place every year that there is not an Olympic Winter Games.

International Growth

The United States and Canada have dominated international women's hockey since the first World Women's Championship in 1990. While those two teams take most of the spotlight at major competitions, other countries have had international success, too.

Finland and Sweden have consistently been the top two teams in Europe. Finland has taken home nine bronze medals at the World Women's Championship. The team has competed for the bronze medal in all 12 championships through 2009. Sweden has competed in the bronze-medal game eight times, winning twice. In the Olympics, Finland has won two bronze medals. Sweden has won a bronze and a silver medal.

China emerged as the top Asian team during the 1990s. The Chinese team finished fourth at the 1998 Olympics. However, few women in China play ice hockey, so the sport is growing slowly. China finished seventh at the 2010 Olympics.

CANADIAN DOMINANCE

Canada was the host country for the first World Women's Championship. Team Canada made sure people would notice them when that tournament was going on. The players wore hot pink jerseys.

The first tournament had a **round-robin** format. Teams from the United States, Canada, Finland, Japan, Norway, Sweden, Switzerland, and West Germany competed for the title of world champion. Canada defeated the United States 5–2 in the gold-medal game.

The 1990 World Championship was the first of eight straight that Canada would win. Team USA took silver in

Canadian Pioneers

Shirley Cameron was a pioneer of Canadian women's hockey. She was one of the original members of the Edmonton Chimos, a women's team organized in 1972. Her competitive career lasted for 20 years. She played in the first World Championship in 1990 and became a coach in 1992.

Defensewoman Judy Diduck played on four of Canada's gold-medal winning teams at the World Championships prior to winning a silver medal at the 1998 Olympics. She started skating as a ringette player, and didn't begin playing hockey until she joined the Edmonton Chimos in the early 1980s.

each of those first eight tournaments. Finland won the bronze medal in seven of the first eight. Canada has led the way in international competition because the sport is very popular in the country, so many girls and women play.

Karyn Bye was a key player for Team USA during six of those silver-medal wins. Bye's total of 51 points in 30 games ranks third in World Women's Championship history. Bye also went on to win gold with Team USA at the 1998 Olympics and silver at the 2002 Olympics.

FIRST CHAMPIONSHIP WIN

In 2005, the U.S. women's team was determined to break through and finally win a gold medal at the World Women's Championship. And that's exactly what they did.

Kim St-Pierre won three Olympic gold medals.

GOLD GALORE

Canadian goalie Kim St-Pierre captured gold medals at the 2002, 2006, and 2010 Olympic Winter Games. In 2008, St-Pierre joined the NHL's Montreal Canadiens during a practice session. She followed Manon Rheaume as the second woman to play with an NHL team, although it was just in practice. Rheaume played in exhibition games with the Tampa Bay Lightning in 1992 and 1993.

Gunn Inspires

Chanda Gunn helped Team USA win the 2005 World Women's Championship. She also earned bronze at the 2006 Olympic Winter Games and silver in the 2007 World Women's Championship. After suffering from seizures as a child, Gunn was diagnosed with epilepsy, a brain disorder that causes seizures, in the fourth grade. She was given medication to control them. She was also careful to get a lot of sleep and avoid stress to prevent seizures. As a result, she has had very few as an adult. She continues to work with epilepsy.com, a Web site that provides information and resources to help those who are affected by the disorder.

Team USA and Canada played to a scoreless tie through regulation and an overtime period. U.S. goaltender Chanda Gunn made 26 **saves**. Canada's Kim St-Pierre made 49.

After overtime, the teams went into a **shootout**. During the shootout, Natalie Darwitz, Angela Ruggiero, and Krissy Wendell scored for Team USA. Sarah Vaillancourt was the only player who scored for the Canadian team. Team USA had finally won its first gold medal at the World Women's Championship.

That 2005 win over Canada boosted the confidence of U.S. players. Team USA went on to win two of the next three World Women's Championship tournaments. After the 2006 Olympics, Team USA took home silver in 2007 and gold in 2008 and 2009.

▲ U.S. goalie Chanda Gunn celebrates after Team USA beat Canada in a shootout to win the 2005 World Women's Championship.

▲ *Women's hockey was welcomed into the Olympics in 1998.*

CHAPTER 5

OLYMPIC
GLORY

Women's hockey reached a major milestone in its development and acceptance as a sport in 1992. That year, the International Olympic Committee voted to include it as a medal sport in the 1998 Olympic Winter Games. It would make its Olympic debut in Nagano, Japan.

THE ROAD TO GOLD

Japanese Olympic officials limited the 1998 Olympic field to six teams: Canada, China, Finland, Japan, Sweden, and the United States. Japan did not have much experience in women's hockey. But it still entered a team because it was the host country.

The top two teams were Canada and the United States. Canada was the strong favorite to win the gold medal. Heading into the 1998 Olympics, Canada had won every World Women's Championship since the tournament began in 1990.

But Team USA was improving. In 1997, the U.S. and Canadian women's teams faced each other 13 times. The teams split victories almost evenly: the United States won six times, and Canada won seven times.

The United States and Canada met during round-robin play in the 1998 Olympics. Canada jumped out to a 4–1 lead midway through the third period. But Team USA scored six unanswered goals to take a 7–4 victory. That gave the U.S. players momentum heading forward.

COMEBACK VICTORY

After round-robin play, Team USA and Canada had the best records. That meant the two favorites would face off in the gold-medal game. Before that game, U.S. coach Ben Smith would not reveal his choice for starting goaltender. Both U.S. goalies had played well throughout the tournament. He had to choose between Sarah Tueting and Sara DeCosta. Smith decided to go with Tueting, from Winnetka, Illinois. She ended up making 21 saves in the gold-medal game.

Team USA forward Gretchen Ulion scored in the second period. That gave her team a 1–0 lead. Teammate Shelley Looney then redirected a shot past Canada's goalie, Manon Rheaume, midway through the third period. Team USA led 2–0. Danielle Goyette scored for Canada with four minutes left to play. But it was not enough. The game was sealed when Team USA's Sandra Whyte scored an empty-net goal to give the U.S. players a 3–1 lead. Canada had pulled its goalie to add an extra forward in the final minutes of the game, leaving the net unguarded.

Pulling the Goalie

Canada pulled its goalie near the end of the 1998 Olympic gold-medal game. "Pulling the goalie" allows a team to continue to play with six players. The goaltender is replaced by a forward, who joins her teammates on the attack. The net is left unguarded because the team is usually losing by a goal or more anyway, so a goal scored by the opponent has no bearing on the result. A loss is a loss whether it is by one goal or more.

▲ Angela Ruggiero skates with the American flag after winning gold at the 1998 Olympics.

Team USA had defeated Canada 3–1 on February 17, 1998, to win the first Olympic gold medal awarded in women's ice hockey.

Shelley Looney

Shelley Looney scored the decisive second goal against Canada in the 1998 Olympic gold-medal game. Her Olympic career also included winning silver in 2002 in Salt Lake City. The Michigan native continued to support the sport after her playing career ended. In 2003, she served as an assistant coach for the boys' National Team Development Program in Ann Arbor, Michigan. She was an assistant coach for the University of Vermont women's team during the 2005–06 season. Looney became the director of women's hockey for the New Jersey Colonials youth hockey organization in 2006.

THE 2002 OLYMPICS

After the upset in the 1998 gold-medal game, the Canadian team was determined to win gold in 2002. But their biggest competition was again Team USA. And this time, Team USA was competing on its home ice in Salt Lake City, Utah.

A field of eight teams competed in Salt Lake City. Team USA won its first-round group. Then it defeated

▲ *Canada's Caroline Ouellette (right) shoots the puck past U.S. defense-woman A. J. Mleczko and goalie Sara DeCosta in the 2002 Olympics.*

Sweden in a semifinal. The gold-medal game found the U.S. and Canadian teams competing again. Team USA came into the game with confidence. The team had defeated the Canadians in their eight meetings leading to the gold-medal game. But that winning streak would end. This time, Canada came out ahead.

Canada's Hayley Wickenheiser scored what would prove to be the winning goal in the second period. That put her team ahead 3–2. Goaltender Kim St-Pierre made 25 saves for Canada. North America's dominance in women's hockey continued. The United States and Canada were now the only teams that had won Olympic gold in women's ice hockey.

Manon Rheaume became the first woman to play with an NHL team.

PLAYING WITH THE MEN

Canadian goalie Manon Rheaume made her first and only appearance at the Olympics in 1998. Approximately six years before, she made the news for another hockey feat. On September 23, 1992, Rheaume became the first and only woman to play in an exhibition game in the NHL. The Tampa Bay Lightning signed her as a free agent. She played in a preseason game against the St. Louis Blues. She returned in 1993 to play for the Lightning in a preseason game against the Boston Bruins.

Rheaume was not the last woman to play professionally with the men. On January 28, 2005, Angela Ruggiero played for the Tulsa Oilers in a Central Hockey League game. She registered one point in the process and became the first woman to play in a regular-season professional hockey game in the United States at a position other than goalie. During the game, she played alongside her brother Bill. He had been a member of the Oilers before his sister joined the team. They became the first brother-sister combination to play professional hockey for the same team at the same time.

AN ALL-AROUND ATHLETE

Krissy Wendell was one player on Team USA in 2002 who could truly be called an all-around athlete. Years before her Olympic debut in Salt Lake City, she competed in the 1994 Little League World Series in Williamsport, Pennsylvania. She was the first female to start a game as catcher in the mostly boys' baseball tournament. Later, Wendell led her Park Center High School hockey team to the 2000 Minnesota state championship. The *Let's Play Hockey* newspaper awarded her the Ms. Hockey award as the state's best player that year.

Next, Wendell served as a captain of the University of Minnesota's women's hockey team. She helped the Golden Gophers win NCAA titles in 2004 and 2005. In 2005, she won the Patty Kazmaier Award as the best player in women's college hockey. Wendell went on to captain the U.S. team at the 2006 Olympic Winter Games.

TURIN 2006

In the 2002 Olympics, the United States and Canada dominated, outscoring their opponents 63–4 before facing off in the gold-medal game. The 2006 Olympic Winter Games in Turin, Italy, were more competitive.

Team USA faced Sweden in the semifinals. The teams were tied at 2–2 after regulation and overtime play. So they went to a shootout. Sweden's goalie Kim Martin had been brilliant during the game. She stopped 37 U.S. shots.

Her strong goaltending continued into the shootout, when she stopped every U.S. shooter. Meanwhile, Sweden scored two goals, advancing to the gold-medal game in one of the biggest upsets in women's hockey history. Sweden went on to lose 4–1 to Canada in the gold-medal game. But it was the first time Sweden had won the silver medal.

Even with the loss to Sweden, the United States still had a chance to win a medal. Team USA played Finland in the bronze-medal game. Katie King scored a **hat trick** to lead the U.S. team to a 4–0 victory and the bronze medal. King was a 30-year-old forward playing in her final Olympics. Her medal-winning performance capped a great career as a hockey player. She had won Olympic gold (1998), silver (2002), and bronze (2006). She completed her international career with 265 points in 210 games. From 1993 to 2001, she won nine consecutive silver medals with Team USA at the World Women's Championship.

Familiar Face in Goal

Following Sweden's upset of the United States in 2006, U.S. players saw a familiar face at the collegiate level. Sweden's Kim Martin, named the top goaltender in the 2006 Olympics, went on to play hockey at the University of Minnesota Duluth.

▲ *Sweden's goalie Kim Martin makes a save during the 2006 Olympics in Turin, Italy.*

Hall of Famers

In 2009, the 1998 U.S. women's Olympic hockey team was inducted into the U.S. Hockey Hall of Fame. Two members of that 1998 team had a good reason for missing the ceremony. Jenny Potter and Angela Ruggiero were busy training for the 2010 Olympic Winter Games.

She also captured gold at that tournament in 2005. King was named head coach of Boston College's women's hockey team in 2007.

After the 2006 Olympics, the U.S. players spent the next four years preparing to get that gold medal back. But Canada was just as determined. The 2010 Olympics were on their home ice.

▲ Team Canada players line up to receive their gold medals at the 2006 Olympics.

▲ Hayley Wickenheiser played with
a Finnish professional men's team in 2003.

CHAPTER 6

PLAY TO WIN

Many girls today have the opportunity to play hockey, whether it be at the youth, college, or Olympic level. Those who make it to the Olympics are considered the best of the best. Not only do they have great talent, but they also must have great passion, fierce determination, and a strong work ethic to compete among the best players in the world.

HAYLEY WICKENHEISER

In 2008, *Sports Illustrated* ranked Canadian Hayley Wickenheiser as the 20th-toughest athlete in the world—male or female. She has done plenty to earn that title during her long career. Wickenheiser was first selected to the Canadian national team at age 15. She has since been named Most Valuable Player of the Olympics twice.

Wickenheiser also proved she could play hockey with the men. She took part in rookie camps with the NHL's Philadelphia Flyers in 1998 and 1999. Then, in 2003, she became the first female hockey player to record a point in a men's professional game. She played a season for a second-division Finnish men's hockey team called Kirkkonummi Salamat. Wickenheiser had two goals and 10 **assists**. Many consider her to be the best female hockey player that Canada has ever produced.

JENNIFER BOTTERILL

Jennifer Botterill is another talented Canadian hockey player. She became a four-time Olympian in 2010. She was the youngest player on the Canadian team that lost to the United States in the 1998 gold-medal game in Nagano, Japan. As a college hockey player at Harvard, Botterill was a two-time winner of the Patty Kazmaier Memorial Award, given to the sport's best player. As of 2010, she was the only player to win the award twice. Botterill is also an accomplished ringette and basketball player.

CAROLINE OUELLETTE

Caroline Ouellette joined Team Canada in 1999. Since then, she has won five gold and three silver medals at the World Championships. Additionally, she was part of gold-medal-winning Olympic teams in 2002 and 2006. Like her teammates Wickenheiser and Botterill, Ouellette was determined to add another Olympic gold in 2010.

Expectations were high leading up to the 2010 Olympics in Vancouver, Canada. It was the first time that the Olympics had been held in the hockey-mad country since women's hockey debuted as an Olympic sport. Many considered Canada to be the favorite. But, as usual, Team USA was not going to make it easy.

NATALIE DARWITZ

Natalie Darwitz counts surfing and juggling among her talents off the ice. But the three-time U.S. Olympian and captain of the 2010 Olympic team also performs magic on the ice. She began her varsity career in the seventh grade, when she began playing on the girls' team at Eagan High School in Minnesota. She averaged nearly five points per game in 102 high school games.

Darwitz had served as captain for three years heading into the 2010 Olympics. During that time, Team USA won the World Women's Championship title in 2008 and 2009. Her speed, creativity, and determination give her the necessary tools to make **havoc** for the opposition.

▲ *(From left to right) Team USA's Julie Chu, Jenny Potter, Jessie Vetter, Natalie Darwitz, and Angela Ruggiero in 2010*

JESSIE VETTER

Jessie Vetter's career at the University of Wisconsin was unmatched. In four years, she played in the NCAA championship game four times, winning it three times. She capped her time there by winning the Patty Kazmaier Award as the top player in women's college hockey.

Vetter tended the net for the U.S. team at the World Women's Championships in 2008 and 2009. The Women's

Sports Foundation named her Sportswoman of the Year in 2009. She was the first ice hockey player to take home that honor.

At the 2010 Olympics, Vetter and Darwitz were determined to bring the gold medal back to the United States.

GOING FOR THE GOLD IN 2010

Team USA and Team Canada breezed through the first round at the 2010 Olympics. Then they each won in the

Patty Kazmaier Memorial Award

The Patty Kazmaier Memorial Award is given to the top college women's hockey player each year. Patty Kazmaier was a defensewoman for Princeton University during the 1980s. She died of a rare blood disease in 1990. The award has been given out since 1998. Three members of the 2010 U.S. Olympic team won the award. They were Angela Ruggiero (2004, Harvard University), Julie Chu (2007, Harvard), and Jessie Vetter (2009, University of Wisconsin). Canadian athletes have won the award five times. The winners were Jennifer Botterill (2001, 2002, Harvard), Sara Bauer (2006, University of Wisconsin), Sarah Vaillancourt (2008, Harvard), and Vicki Bendus (2010, Mercyhurst College).

semifinals. The much-awaited final matchup was set: USA versus Canada for the gold medal. Canada's Wickenheiser had lived up to the hype at the Olympics. The four-time Olympian became the all-time leading scorer in Olympic history. Meanwhile, Darwitz had seven assists and four goals for Team USA. But there was one thing both women wanted and only one would get: the gold medal.

The arena was packed for the gold-medal game. It was the largest crowd ever for a women's hockey game. Most of the fans were wearing red in support of the Canadian national team. The arena was loud. But the U.S. players did their best to focus and play hard.

Canada's Marie-Philip Poulin scored two goals in the first period. But after that, Vetter was like a brick wall. Team USA's defense held up for the rest of the game. Forward Julie Chu even dove across the ice to stop shots with her body. But the usually strong U.S. offense could not get the puck past Canada's goalie. In the end, it was the result that the hometown fans wanted to see. Canada had won 2–0.

Darwitz, Vetter, and their U.S. teammates were disappointed. They had worked very hard to prepare for the 2010 Olympics. Their effort had shown in the gold-medal game. Even the Canadian fans recognized it. After the game, the Canadian fans showed their respect for the team by loudly chanting, "U-S-A! U-S-A!"

Clarkson Cup

Like Lord Stanley, Adrienne Clarkson was a governor general in Canada (1999–2005). Also like Stanley, Clarkson lent her name to a hockey trophy. The Clarkson Cup is given to the top women's club team in North America. The first Clarkson Cup was awarded to Team Canada after it won gold at the 2006 Olympics. Beginning in 2009, the Cup has been awarded to the best team from Canadian Women's Hockey League and the Western Women's Hockey League. Many of the top players from the U.S. and Canadian national teams play in those hockey leagues when not playing with their national or college teams.

BRIGHT FUTURE

Team USA brought 21 women to the 2010 Olympics. Of them, 15 were first-time Olympians. Three U.S. players—Hilary Knight and twins Jocelyne and Monique Lamoureux—were only 20 years old. Despite their youth, all three were among Team USA's top players in the tournament.

Two young players starred for Team Canada, as well. Poulin, who scored both goals in the gold-medal game, was the youngest player on the team. She was only 18. The next youngest player, at age 20, was forward Rebecca Johnston. She had one goal and five assists in the 2010 Olympics.

▲ *Today, young girls like this one can grow up dreaming of winning the Clarkson Cup.*

Soon after the world's top players competed at the 2010 Olympic Winter Games, the 2010 Under-18 World Championships showcased some of the world's top young players. Brigette Lacquette and Jessica Campbell starred for Team Canada, which won the gold medal. Lacquette was named the tournament's best defensewoman, and Campbell was named the Most Valuable Player. Campbell scored seven goals and had eight assists for 15 points in five games.

Team USA finished with a silver medal. American Kendall Coyne led the tournament with 10 goals and was named the top forward of the event. Alex Rigsby of Team USA was selected as the tournament's top goaltender. For third-place Sweden, Lisa Hedengren led the team with three goals and three assists.

Some of the players on these teams are expected to take over for Botterill, Potter, Ruggiero, and Wickenheiser as the next superstars of women's hockey. Some of the other future stars might today only be known to their peewee teammates. But with the growth of girls' and women's hockey on all levels, the sport is only getting more exciting. There is no better time to start playing hockey!

▲ Hilary Knight takes a shot against Canada in a 2010 exhibition game.

GLOSSARY

amateur: Refers to athletes who have never competed for money.

assists: The pass or passes that set up a goal. Also, the point given to the player whose pass leads to a goal (up to two awarded).

back-check: When a player skates toward her goal to defend it against an opponent.

backhand: A shot or pass taken from the outside area of a hockey stick's blade.

blocker: A rectangular goalie pad worn over the hand that holds the stick. It is used to deflect shots hit to that side of the body.

boards: Walls around the outside of the rink that keep the puck from going out of play.

debuted: When something or someone first appeared.

defensewoman: A player who tries to stop players on the opposing team from scoring and typically stands on the offensive blue line. They can also score goals, but are not in the first line of offense.

face-offs: Plays that start or restart action in a hockey game. Two opposing players meet in the middle and the referee drops the puck between them, with the winner hitting the puck to a teammate to start the play.

forehand: A shot or pass taken from the inside or curved area of a hockey stick's blade.

forwards: Players who control the puck and try to score goals. The left wing, right wing, and center are forwards.

goaltender: The player who stands in front of the goal and tries to prevent the puck from entering.

hat trick: When an individual player scores three goals in a single game, it is called a hat trick.

havoc: Disruption or chaos.

hockey sticks: Usually made out of wood, aluminum, or graphite, they have a long, rectangular shaft with a flat blade at the end that is used to shoot, stick-handle, and pass the puck.

National Hockey League (NHL): The top professional hockey league in North America.

penalty: A rule violation that requires a player to leave the ice for a certain amount of time, usually two minutes.

puck: A small, black disc made out of rubber that is about an inch thick and three inches wide.

rink: The ice sheet on which hockey is played. It is surrounded by boards to keep the puck in play.

round-robin: A format in which every team plays each other at least once.

saves: Shots that are blocked by the goaltender.

shootout: A way to determine a winner in a game that is tied after overtime. In the Olympics, five players from each team alternately take shots on a goal defended only by a goaltender.

shot: The act of hitting the puck toward the net.

FOR MORE
INFORMATION

BOOKS

Avery, Joanna, and Julie Stevens. *Too Many Men on the Ice: Women's Hockey in North America*. Custer, WA: Polestar, 1997.
A history of women's hockey.

MacDonald, James. *Hockey Skills: How to Play Like a Pro*. Berkeley Heights, NJ: Enslow, 2009.
A how-to guide to playing hockey.

Ruggiero, Angela. *Breaking the Ice: My Journey to Olympic Hockey, the Ivy League & Beyond*. Plymouth, MA: Drummond, 2005.
The story of Angela Ruggiero's life playing hockey, from her childhood in California to Harvard to the Olympics.

Turco, Mary. *Crashing the Net: The U.S. Women's Olympic Hockey Team and the Road to Gold*. New York: HarperCollins, 1999.
The story of the first U.S. Olympic women's hockey team and how it won a gold medal at the 1998 Olympics.

USA Hockey Coaching Education Program, Level 1 — Skill Development Manual. Colorado Springs, CO: USA Hockey, 1995.
A guide to playing hockey for beginners.

WEB SITES

Canadian Women's Hockey League
http://cwhl.ca/
This Web site has official schedules, rosters, stats, and more from the Canadian Women's Hockey League.

KidsHealth
Winter Sports: Sledding, Skiing, Snowboarding, Skating
http://kidshealth.org/kid/watch/out/winter_sports.html
This Web site features information about staying safe while having fun with winter sports.

KidzWorld
Cammi Granato biography
http://www.kidzworld.com/article/1543-cammi-granato-biography
A bio of former U.S. hockey star Cammi Granato.

PBS Kids
Kids World Sports
http://pbskids.org/kws/sports/icehockey.html
An overview of ice hockey.

USA Hockey
http://www.usahockey.com/
The Web site for the national governing body for hockey in the United States offers information on U.S. hockey, from youth hockey through the U.S. national teams.

The Women's Hockey Web
http://www.whockey.com/
An online resource for everything about women's hockey.

INDEX

PLACES TO VISIT

Hockey Hall of Fame

30 Yonge Street
Toronto, ON, Canada M5E 1X8
(416) 360-7735
www.hhof.com
The Hockey Hall of Fame features a large collection of hockey memorabilia—including the Stanley Cup—as well as interactive exhibits, games, and theaters.

U.S. Hockey Hall of Fame

801 Hat Trick Avenue
Eveleth, MN 55734-8640
(218) 744-5167
www.ushockeyhall.com
The U.S. Hockey Hall of Fame features exhibits, videos, and memorabilia that highlight the people who helped hockey grow in the United States.

ABOUT THE AUTHOR

Dave McMahon has covered girls' and women's hockey at all levels. A former editor of *Let's Play Hockey* in Minneapolis, Minnesota, he has also written hockey stories for USA Hockey and the Minnesota Wild. He lives in Eagan, Minnesota, with his wife and three hockey-playing children.

ABOUT THE CONTENT CONSULTANT

Angela Ruggiero is one of only two players to compete in the first four Olympic hockey tournaments for Team USA. During the Vancouver 2010 Olympic Winter Games, Ruggiero was also elected to the International Olympic Committee Athletes' Commission.